Waqar Aamir Katiar

We are Weird

60 Weird habits, Reasons and Ways to Break

To Lovely Land (Earth) & My Mother, Both teach me

Table of Contents

28. Not Shaving Daily
29. Try to Park in Small Space
30. Study in Last Days
31. Smelling Own Breath after Wake up
32. Arguments are for thinking, Not for Saying
33. Adding Sugar in Green Tea
34. Talking to Yourself
35. Books for showing, not for reading
36. Foods Battle
37. Name Things we use
38. Touching with Both
39. Listening Music while Working
40. Talking to Things
41. Holding Glass for Long Time
42. Criticize everything
43. Brushing Teeth for Long Time
44. Watching same Movies/Episode again and again
45. Reading Shampoo Back Cover under Shower
46. Check then leave home
47. Sleeping at parties
48. Examine money
49. Forget spelling of Simple Words
50. Extra Kind on Social Media
51. Use both hands to drink a Glass of Water
52. Laughing without any Reason
53. Not replying to Phone calls
54. Licking before eating
55. Buying small size of Shoes, they look better
56. Wearing 2 watches, holding 2 cell phones
57. After Reading few pages, Saying I read whole book
58. Saying twice at Call, Saying Loudly
59. Change Plan
60. Forget to switch off TV

Preface

After cleaning nose we see tissue paper, may be nose drips diamonds.
While sitting in a conference, putting hand in pocket and be sure about existence of cellphone. Maybe having a threat of theft from CEO, sitting next to you.

These are examples of we are weird. I decided to write about our weird habits and describe logic and reasons behind these. How to break these habits too. I am also a weird person. I admit it. May be I am the most weird person in the world. Be realistic and honest about life, don't be artificial like a robot. I try to make you happy and give some knowledge in this book. Hope you will enjoy reading

I am 37 now, have you noticed my sentence? Read it again, if I write I am 37? Is it make sense? Or should I add 1 more word to make more authenticate you and me that I am talking about this time? I am 37 is enough, no need to write now, may be due to my habit or make more sense I written now with it
This is called we are weird, we always do such meaningless activities and things in our lives that we shouldn't do. In this book we will learn and try to understand about such weird things and reasons behind these and how we avoid them. We see and observe many things in daily life. We try to improve our living at home, office or at a bar. We try to adopt good habits and practices to make us more and more mistake less. Its human nature to keep improving living from dark ages to this highly sophisticated technology based homes.

We generally do some weird things in our daily life like, we see our smartphone after few minutes even we have no new notification, and sometimes we laugh at ourselves and on others too. It doesn't matter how educated or experienced we are. I noticed myself once after doing a weird mistake, I was alone so I stopped working and I started thinking about it. I finalized to go home and list down such things and try to avoid in future about them. I list it, thought and discuss with my friends about these things. I realized to write these weird mistakes we usually do and how we should avoid them, I decided to write in a book form because a blog or article in newspaper or magazine may be we lost them easily. We read blogs, we learn from them but if we have habit of reading blogs according to our need then we won't remember name of it. Usually a book is always in our shelf or at our hard disk. It's easy to find it.This book is very easy to understand, second thing is about our way of improving, we are masterpiece of nature, we are humans, we can do anything and can control on critical conditions too. Just having aim of it. Keep in mind that these habits are not a big issue and in few weeks we will break them.

I try to make this book every easy so a child and old man can enjoy and understand at same level. I divide this book in deferent chapters according to weird habits, these habits are according to frequency of them in our lives means how these have strong influence on us, I describe logic behind to do it and how we avoid it. I am not a professional writer, I write few articles in local newspapers and this is my first book, I apologize for my mistakes, not weird in this book. I always welcome your feedback.

Yours
Waqar Aamir Katiar,
@waqaraamrkatiar

Acknowledgment

I learned from life and land, on I am living. I thank to you people and nature, who teach me a lot. I hope you all will teach me as you do. ☺
These all experiences and techniques to break weird habits are learnt from this world and creatures of it. I want to deliver my contribution to world and humanity in form of this book.

Important Note to Reader

Dear Reader,
I have written this book after breaking my weird habits and I hope you too. I want to suggest you to maintain a diary for your routine activities and write all plans and activities you have to do and when you finish an activity, mark it like that

~~Finishing Book "We are Weird"~~
~~Going to eat Pizza with Friends~~
~~Buying new shirts~~
Buying Shoes
Buying Sunglasses
~~Ironing Clothes for next week~~

This is an easy way to do activities according to your plan and time period. You have clear in mind, only 2 activities you need to do, for example, buying shoes and sunglasses. You buy them as soon as possible because you need to mark and finish all activities and move to next list of activities because life is moving forward and we have to do new activities according to our needs. Try to develop habit of maintain diary and write list of activities and mark after finishing. Analyze your performance after a month, how much you done in this month and how much activities are still remaining. Don't start next month activities before finish this month remaining activities. I promise you, you will get whatever you write on paper and you save your time and money by managing yourself properly.

1. **Selfies kill**

16th July 2017, Chennai, India

48 People were injured taking selfies. In Chennai these 48 people were standing close to a burning bakery and they ignored warning them to move away from that place

11 June 2017, Russia

4 kids killed by train while taking selfies on railway line.

It's a fact. Smoking kills, Selfies too. These are just 2 examples about our weird habit of taking selfies at very dangerous places. Many people injured and died every year. We know the risk factor but we neglect it. Why? Why we do it even we know we could be injured? Reason behind this weird habit is we always calculate a margin of safety in these situations, a margin of distance or margin of safety we have in our minds. We know we can run, jump or move quickly from that space, area or place. Yes, we can do. We have abilities and experience of handling such situations. Sometimes we neglect other factors like nature of incident like flood, rain, and fire e-t-c, volume and intensity like earthquake, tsunami, at a very high place, in storms, twisters, and heavy rains cause floods. In such situations we could face trouble. We can't measure intensity and uncertainty of that movement. We always find excitement and adventure in such situations and we want to share these movements to others who are not being a part of that movement so we try to capture it in our cameras for forever.

How to break this habit? It's very simple, you need to do

- Read injuries and causalities incidents happened while selfie taking, you will understand selfie kills, it's our nature to avoid dangerous things and activities

- Slow down your frequency of posting selfies on social media, if you are posting 10 Or 5 selfies a day, you should slowly reduce this quantity and try to post 1 selfie a day, if you are posting 1 selfie per day, you need to post it 1 or 2 days later. This is a method to reduce selfie taking habit and when you have control on posting and taking selfies, you won't take risk.
- Take only 1 picture for selfie, we want to look better and beautiful, we take 10 pics and post 1. This habit make us selfies addict. We should take only 1 picture. Try to change this habit. It's an easy way to do it is never upload pic from gallery, always take from camera, Facebook, Twitter, WhatsApp and other apps have this option, take and post directly. This method will reduce to take more selfies
- Watch TV first, watch forecast about intensity and nature of rain, storm and fire
- Don't go there if officially warned people to be there
- Don't take selfies on railway lines, high mountains, near waterfalls, sitting on trees

These are few techniques and tips to break this weird habit. I hope we can break this habit. Be careful and Love your life because life is beautiful.

2. Energy Drink after Gym

One of my best friend is overweight, he is 36 and having 231 lbs. or 104 Kg, he has been exercising for few months but his weight is still same. I usually see him after coming from gym, he has wet shirt and tired body. I asked him several times about his weight, he always tells the same weight, and I shocked every time. One day I decided to go with him to gym and see about his workout. I went, saw him. He started with breathing exercise for warmup, he start to lift him for warmup body, then he started different exercises according to his plan. He exercised about 50 minutes and he and his cloths were wet. After finishing exercise, he drunk energy drink, and flavored juice. I hadn't any idea about calories and sugar quantity added in these type of drink. I asked his instructor, about his weight losing program, he said that he prohibited him to not drink these drinks because they have high quantity of sugar level and calories he burnt will increase after drinking drinks, so, result will be nothing. I have seen few other people in my life they drink these drinks and they gain weight instead of losing. You can search on google about sports and energy drink, a famous sports drink contains 76 grams of sugar, 12 grams per 100 ml and in 600 ml packing bottle it has 72 grams of sugar.

72 grams sugar = 280 calories

1 hour gym workout = burn 350 calories

If we take difference 350 calories losing after gym workout – 280 calories from drink = 70 calories

We lose only 70 calories per day if we exercise and drink high sugar energy drinks.

According to Dr. Max Wishnofsky in 1958, said that 1 pound or Lbs. of human body have 3500 calories. It means if we want to lose 1 Lbs. or pound (454 grams) of our body weight, we should burn 3500 calories.

Keep in mind above case, he was just loosing 70 calories in 1 day, so,

He need to exercise 3500/70 = 50 days

That was the reason of his same weight after exercise daily. If he exercise this way 365 days (1 year)

70 x 365 = 25,550 calories. Divide 25550 by 3500 = 7.3 lbs or 3.3 kgs weight loss in 1 year.

If you are trying to lose your weight, please don't take high sugar drinks and foods. All will increase your weight. This our habit of taking soft drinks with meal and energy drinks after workout, this weird habit will give us more weight gain instead of losing it. Don't drink and completely say no to these. If you really want to lose weight, try this formula and you will definitely lose weight. Don't take any artificial type of sugar in drinks and foods. Avoid artificial sugar drinks and foods completely. Don't stop sugar consumption completely because our body needs sugar and decrease in sugar levels may increase some other health issues. Take natural sugar sources like fruits and juices. You will fell a difference. I tries it myself and I get difference. Take a simple example from below calculation

If we drink a 600ml soft drink bottle a day, it has 278 calories

In 1 month we drink 278 x 30 = 8340 calories

8340/3500 = 2.38 Lbs. or pounds per months

It's very simple to lose 2.4 Lbs in 1 month just not to drink 1 soft drink bottle daily without any exercise.

3.   Order more, Eat Less

Have you ever noticed how much time a grain takes to be a plant and give grains? Have you ever noticed how much efforts a farmer do to protect crops from pests and animals? Have you noticed how many nights a farmer not sleep and look after crops? We have no idea if we are living in urban areas or cities.

It's a long and difficult process of agriculture, a grain to pancake or a pizza is a result of efforts of months of human and nature. Be thankful to nature and love land for delicious fruits and healthy vegetables and grains.

According to research **Americans waste 150,000 Tones food per day**, if we convert it in Kgs it will be 150 million Kgs per day. Imagine how much cost it, and how many poor and Hungary people can eat it. Most of in these items are fruits, vegetables and fast food items. Imagine this figure is only in America, rest of world is more and higher in numbers than America. We 4 persons on table we order of 6. We can't eat as much as of 5 person and 1 person food remain on table. We pay this person amount without eating it. We pay it every day and we are going to lost money every day and if we calculate it on monthly or early basis the loss will be in thousand dollars and this food is not served to needy Hungary poor people. If you have this weird habit of losing money this way then you should donate this money to orphanage or shelter and help to people. This habit is very common among us. We don't care while ordering food and we have no idea about wastage of food. It's very simple to avoid this weird habit. We need to do

- Know about our eating habits and times
- Know about quantity we can easily eat like, number of items in terms of single items and combination of different Items
- Calculate items consumption per person, its may be difficult but we should know about our family at least, how many Pizzas are require for our whole family, how many burgers our family can easily eat, how many pizzas and burgers our family need for dinner.
- Don't order completely if you have no idea about guests, order 80% according to your estimates about quantity of people and items, order in between eating

and chatting with guests according to remaining needs of guests and your family

- Keep in mind quantity of people and items in mind and set a budget, don't go restaurant with credit cards and keep few dollars more cash than food budget to restaurant.

After practicing these techniques you will never order more food and you will save your precious money and food wastage.

4. Sleeping after wake up (Alarm for sleep)

It was one of my bad habit , wakeup in morning and seeing time, oh its 5:45, I have to wake up on 6:00 so I have 15 minutes more to sleep, I sleep and when I wake up its 7:45. All schedule of day ruins. I faced so much embarrassment with this weird habit. The reason behind this weird habit is usually in morning it's difficult to leave bed especially in winter. We think we have 15 or 20 minutes and we plan to sleep just few minutes more but our sleeping habit make it long and we wake up after completing our whole sleep time. We need at least 6 to 8 hours sleep every day, our body and mind wants to complete this amount of time at any cost, if we sleep late in night and try to wake up in early morning so it's too difficult to leave bed easily. This weird habit is due to late night gatherings, social media or internet surfing. Such activities take much time and we are completely mentally involved in surfing or participating in these and us unaware of time and sleep. We sleep late and wake up late. To avoid this weird habit we have to do these simple ways.

First one is to see our life pattern, like

Average time to reach at our office or academy time

Average time we need to prepare in morning.

Average time required in traveling to reach office or academy

Average our sleep time (may vary from person to person, 6 hours to 8 hours)

Let's suppose we have to reach office at 9:00 AM, we take 1 hour time in preparing ourselves in morning before leaving home to office, time include breakfast too. We need average 30 minutes to reach office

From above information, we need 1 hour 30 minutes after wake up to reach office. So we have to wake up at 7:30 at any cost. And if sleep time is 8 hours so we should sleep at 11:30 PM and wake up 7:30 AM, if sleep time is 7 hours, we need to sleep at least before 12:30 AM. Don't be at any gathering or on internet after 12:30 AM, must be in on bed at this time. Because **we need 7 our 8 hours of sleep to wake up automatically** and if we sleep 2 hours late than defiantly we need more 2 hours to complete sleep time, so we face difficulty to wake up 2 hours before sleep time. If we wake up at 7:30 and we have 2 hours gap in sleep so, definitely we try to sleep few minutes and keep in mind that we just sleep for 15 minutes but these 15 minutes will be 150 minutes. How to avoid this weird habit. It's very simple

- Set alarm for sleep, it means you have in mind your wake up time plus sleeping hours. clock 15 minutes before sleep if you are at home and if you are in a gathering then set it 30 minutes before sleep time because you need to reach home and change clothes or taking bath
- if want to wake up at 7:30 set alarm at 7:15 and leave some your work pending like shoe polishing, pressing clothes or some official work, you have in mind that you have to finish remaining work and to do press clothes or

polishing shoes so you get up after wakeup and finish all remaining tasks.

I tried this strategy and I broke this worst and weird habit in few weeks. I believe you will be able to do it easily.

5. Buying in Bulk

Salesgirl: Welcome Sir!

Me: thanks

Salesgirl: Sir we have a very good saving offer for you

Me: sure

Salesgirl: if you buy this 1 noddle packet its $2, if you buy 10 it will be $17 or 1.7 per packet and if you buy 20 packets you will get it $32

Me: give me 20 packets

I bought 20 packets of noodles. I usually east 2 packets in a month because I eat it to change my routine and for change my taste. I bought 10 months quantity at once to save my 8 dollars or you can say 4 additional packets of noodles. I eat them as I do and after 4 months I noticed that packets are near to be expired or expiry date is near. What should I do? Should I eat them every day to finish them or I bear loss? This is happened with me several times and I lost money. This is a weird habit that lost your precious money, precious because you have done lot of efforts to earn it. **We see temporary benefits while we shopping and we don't keep in mind** about our consumptions and we not consumed items completely before expiring. It's very simple to break this habit. What we need is

- List down items monthly consumptions in respect of quantity
- List down items you use frequently like shampoo, soap, detergent and oil e-t-c
- List down items not you use regularly or once in a month
- List down items you need in quarter or semi annually

At shopping you should have this list or keep in mind about items quantity and need. You may buy in bulk quantity of items having expiring date is in years like soaps and detergents but edible items have short term expire period so buy according to time of expiry and according to your needs. No need to grab items to save just few dollars and buying in huge quantity because you will not use all items and you lost your money. Don't go to discounts because companies have to sell more and more quantities to gain more profits and they don't have any sympathy to customers and loss of them

6.   Washing Hands Continuously

Cats' family (Loins and cats) clean them more and more after eating, we are not cats but we do it. If you ever touched with a dirty thing like used baby diaper or such dirty things, you quickly go to wash out your hands, you wash them continuously even after cleaned, it's very important to you in respect of hygiene factor but if someone is looking you, maybe he thinks strange about you. We never easily satisfy after washing once after getting dirty from gutter water or something like that. We want to wash again and again to washout our dirtiness. Stop washing again and again, 2 times is enough for us. Take plastic disposable gloves while working in such situations and wash only 2 times. Make a rule in mind that 02 times is enough. Don't wash them more than that limit. After few weeks of this practice you will won't wash them more and more times.

7. Too Wordy

Teacher: have you done your homework?

Student: Actually, when I reach home, my dog was not at home, we all family members were busy in finding it and we found it late night. I was tired and slept. So, I didn't do homework

Teacher: I asked in yes or No, not asked whole story

Student: actually, I wanted to say no, but I thought tell you reason of not doing my homework.

We generally talk irrelevant words and sentences and we think we are talking properly. It's very awkward if we talk too many words instead of single word like yes or no. This weird habit is very bad when you giving interview. Employers dislike talkative employees. They believe talkative people are less productive and they waste their own and others time in unnecessary talks and emails. Employers also like people who talk in short sentences and words because mostly communication in organization is based on emails and if you have weird habit of writing long sentences and long emails may be you won't get better position or designation in same or other organization. Reason behind this habit is when we feel our statement is not proper or complete then we try to make it strong by adding facts, numbers and other things. We make it long and we feel confident about it after making it long and strong. We want to tell whole once. To break this habit, do simple exercises. I tried these exercises and I get results within 30 days after starting these simple exercises

- Describe yourself, family members and friends in 1 sentence. Write only 1 line for everyone you like. Write reason, why you like him or her
- Define yourself, family members and friends in 1 word
- Write about your best vacations in 1 page essay
- Write summary about your favorite movies and books. Not more than 1 page
- Reply to text massages in few words, not more than 10 words per reply

8. Smelling books, socks, shoes and nails

We generally smell old and unused books maybe we calculate age of these books by smelling instead of reading publication date. Similarly after long walks or coming from a marathon, we smell our shoes and socks may be we calculate distance or calories burned by smell. It is too weird in public so, we do it at home when we alone. Socks and shoes smell bad, because our swat, more walking means more swatting, after long walks we have in mind our swat. We think as more walk as more swat, so we smell socks to see how much we worked out today. Similarly we smell nails after cutting. May be we want to know about how these are dirty inside. It's very easy to avoid smelling books, shoes and socks, clean books dirt after taking it from shelf, clean dust, see publication date, it doesn't matter when you purchased because the day book published its date of birth of it. Age of book you get by this way. Take a smart watch or app in cell phone to count distance or calories you burned. If you have not smartwatch or smartphone walk or run on highways where distance marking is available. You will easily know how much miles you done. **I don't wanted to add it but one more thing we do with our undergarments too**, I have no logic in my mind to describe it because some of us do it and have no logic and reason of it. It's very difficult to avoid it because it only done in washroom or when we alone so we have no issue to do it but maybe we can avoid this habit by not staying more time in washroom or bedroom while changing clothes, we put coffee in mug or place food in oven and go to change clothes so we have in mind that we have only few minutes and have to take coffee or meal. Or do some work in pending and have to continue or complete after changing clothes. Nature of that work should be very quick to finish, like food in oven, tea or coffee making, e-t-c. I believe you will break this habit soon

9. Watching cell phone with no notification

Mostly teens and adults have this weird habit, even at a party or public gathering they watch and watch it again and again. Most of them have boyfriend/girlfriends and with very strong bounding of love and affection. They can't live without each other. This habit make them weird in public. Even on bed they watch and watch cell phone before sleep and they wake up late in morning. In addition people who involved strongly at social media are also have this habit. Breaking this habit is so simple. First one is if you can wear shirt with button flap pocket, or wear pants or jeans with such type of pockets. Keep button closed. When you try to watch notifications you have to open and close button after taking off cellphone and when you put inside, you need to open and close button again and again or shirt. You don't want to open and close button again and again, after few hours your frequency will decrease gradually and after few days you will only watch cell phone when it rings.

10. Read again and again Sent Items

I had this weird habit, I lost my time by this weird mistake. Usually in office I did it. Even I was doing very important work. Similarly I watched text messages I sent. Both had logics. My designation is very critical at office, I have to reply emails with very care and attention. One bad or unnecessary word could make trouble. I read emails before sent and read sent items after mailing. I uploaded method of naming on scribd.com I received many calls and emails from across globe. I tell them first alphabet of name according to name and sometimes full name. Aftersent text message I read again message to ensure about my calculations because these should be accurate and little mistake can make a difference. I wasted my time in these 2 weird habits. Few times my colleague laughed at me after seeing my reading sent emails. It was very difficult for me to break these habits but one day I read a blog about this habit and I started working on itI broke it in 2 months. It's very simple. You email and go outside from room or office for drinking water or to talk to someone at office. You should close email window before leaving seat. Come and start other work on pc not login to email, login after 10 minutes and don't see sent items button. It's very difficult at start but you do it. First few days will be more painful and difficult but gradually you will break it, because go outside again and again is not possible for you when you have lot of work so you naturally avoid it.

11. Add Movies, not for watching

YouTube is like a universe and university. You can entertain and be informed by it. From Tutorials and tips to songs and soaps are all available. I learnt many skills from YouTube and this books you are reading now is also an inspiration and idea I got from YouTube. When you analysis audience of YouTube, you will find a large number of viewers are like to watch movies on YouTube because of its free and if you don't like movie you may skip it and watch another movies. In cinema you buy ticket and if you don't like movie you have no option to lose money and go to home, no option for replacement for movies in cinema. We love YouTube for its huge collection of movies. We watch and enjoy it. We are very easy to see movies on cellphone and tablets due to handle device in hand. Before sleep we like to watch movies on YouTube.

When we see movie on YouTube we have more movies in list with movie we are watching, YouTube provide list of similar movies with currently playing movie and we have option to see other movies of same actors or subject. This feature is very helpful to complete collection and to have more movies for you. In addition you have option to add movies in watch it letter and see them after current movie or on another time. this feature is very helpful but when we watch a movie and click on other movie and click on watch it letter and then go to again on current movie you were watching few seconds ago, and if you frequently doing this again and again then you have a big list of movies for watching. On daily basis if we are adding only 5 movies then we have 150 movies in a month in watch it letter list and if we watch 1 movie daily, because we can't watch 2 movies daily due to length of time. We will only watch 30 movies and 120 movies will remain in list and 120 will be included in next month so 1440 movies in a year. **I guarantee you, you won't finish your list in your whole life** because this weird habit will adding and adding and you won't have enough time to watch 5 or 10 movies a day even on weekends too.

To break this weird habit you just need to do

- Don't switch from one movie to other movie while you are watching it, because if you switch to other movie

and you forward few scenes and you will click on watch
it letter list.

- Don't set a goal to complete collection of a actor or
  subject by watching all relevant movies, just keep in
  mind about subject or actor and have to only watch 1
  movie per day
- Complete your collection on the basis or actors or
  subjects, don't be so hurry
- Set a target on surfing on YouTube, like 2 hours or 3
  hours which is comfortable to your schedule and don't
  surf more then it
- If you have to watch movies on immediately basis,
  manually list down movies list and search and watch it
  and mark name in list. Don't make list in PC or in your
  favorites.

12. Keeping clothes, shoes and watches

I have 15 pairs of shoes, 12 watches and 20 shirts now. I think I
have more than enough stuff. 1 watch is enough seeing time. 2
pairs of shoes are enough to live well and 7 shirts are enough if I
change shirt every day. I know about my life style and these are
more then I need. May be you have this weird habit too. Logic
behind my stuff is buying attractive things like shoes and
watches. Once I see my favorite brand item with new design or
with attractive color, I like to buy it. I don't care about money
because I have debit and credit card so if I have not enough
money to buy it then I use my credit card but I buy it at any
cost. I have 1 Swiss watch and 11 Japanese watches. Whenever I
like a watch I try to buy it and it also happens with shoes and
shirts. I don't wear these regularly but having it. Few watches
from these I only worn once when I bought them and now these
are not in use. Why I spent huge amount on shoes and
watches? Will I will wear them? I have no answers to these

questions but I broke this habit just about few months ago. It's too difficult for girls and women but if they try definitely they break this weird habit.

- Try to make saving habit like make a plan of save a certain amount in bank account, buy an insurance policy, you will get more and more on maturity or invest in stock markets
- List down items you don't need more, like if you have 12 watches now don't buy till you use all
- Budget your income in portions like food, bills, entertainment and don't cross limits of these portions
- Don't go to shopping centers without any need
- Bring a list of items to shopping, buy only listed items
- Don't move to different sections of shopping center

13. Doing Double

Most of us try to through cane in dustbin from a distance, mostly we failed to put it inside. We walk again and put it in properly. We done double work instead of we just walk and put it in. we know about our skills **and we also know this skill is not good so we do double work instead of single.**

Malcolm Gladwell a famous writer, written in his book a 10,000 hours formula of practice. He described if we work on a single skill for 10000 hours then we become master in that skill and always give 100% result. We see in TV programs, such skills like putting card in a box from distance, hitting an object by ball from distance or landing paper aero plane at a target. These people have high skills and they have huge experience of practice but we have no experience of it any we mostly unable to put cane in dustbin. We have 2 options to break this habit. First one is to avoid through and second one is to mark 10000 hours practice. Definitely you chose first one because you have not enough time to do such things and waste your time in practicing to through objects in dustbin. Performers are professionals and they have to do practice because it's earning source of them not for you. Avoid to put from a distance, walk and put it.

14. Wishing birthday next day

If your birthday in on 25th and your best friend wish you on 27[th]or on 26[th]what you feel? It's bad and worst if your girlfriend or boyfriend do it. Life is moving so fast. We forget many daily routine tasks and birthdays are very difficult to remember and if we know birthday but we forget it to wish on the day of it. Due to our busy schedule we forget to wish birthdays to our family members too. Only 1 day we celebrate in whole year with joy and sprit, which is only dedicated to us. We happy more if more people wish us. Especially our best friends and relatives. If you have this habit like I have, to forget wishing birthdays on time. Don't worry you can break it easily by

- List down all friends and relatives and family members' birthdays, if you have problem then collect this data from Facebook.
- Set reminders and alarms in cellphone or in your digital calendars. You will get notifications
- Try to use Facebook daily, because it shows birthdays of current day.

15. Same CV (Resume) for every Job

We are career oriented professionals, it's very difficult to survive in corporate world without upgrading skills and going upward in respect of designations and salary. We switch jobs and organizations for our better future. We want to earn more and try to make more sustainable position in organization or career. When we try to switch for other job we submit our resume. We forget to update resume and we just mail or upload it without updating. Now you may think about need of update. Why we should update. Answer is very simple. We should write our skills according to organization. For example I have teaching and accountant experience so if I am applying job for a teacher again from accountant job in my career then I should mention my teaching experience first and with more emphasize on words and data related to teaching not to accounting. Organizations focus on relevant field education and experience. They don't hire from other field professionals like textile accountant is not easily can get job in a paint factory, because he don't know about many terms of that industry and employer won't take risk to hire him, because he will take time to understand terminologies and industry practices. It's better for us to update resume before applying for a new job and update it with most close relevant skills require for that job. If we apply with old resume than we will lose a chance and time too. Use new resume templets to make your resume more and more attractive and comprehensive for employer and make you different from other candidates by using few efforts. I hope you will definitely get job easily if you adopt this technique. To break this habit, read Job Descriptions of the job you are applying, note key requirements and mention in resume according to requirements.

16. Saying yes

I faced much trouble by saying yes to people for different type of tasks when I was teenager. Like if I am preparing for my exams and someone saying me to write an essay for him, or make assignment of him, I always say yes. When he given me task, I leave my preparation and start his work, I lost my time and efforts. I lost my time and I realized after few years that I didn't do well. This is not fair with ourselves if we leave our important works for other people. I don't want to stop you from helping to people. I just wanted you to realize how important is your education, career and life. You are first for yourself. You need your time, efforts and money first then others. Say yes when you have time and you can easily do it. Few tips for breaking this weird habit are

- List down your daily duties and tasks
- List down your activities on weekends
- Calculate your free time, means when you have no activity or work
- Keep in mind that free time and utilize that time in social causes like helping other people

17. Credit Card Cage

Credit card are now a necessity of our life, we can move and buy without money. We have no worries in last dates of month and not to ask from family and friends about financial help in terms of lending or borrowing money, yes we return this money to them but it's a shameful movement when we ask for it. Credit cards solved this issue and now we are not shameful. Credit cards have limit of amount it's according to nature and type of customer. Customer need to pay a minimum amount in installments to pay back if he can't pay whole amount. Interest-free periods are also include credit cards payments, these periods vary to banks and countries regulatory authorities. If you settled your amount within these days, you won't pay more than the amount you spend, no interest will be charged. You may have more than 1 credit card. Credit cards decide your limits of purchasing because your data of income allows you limits of consumptions. You can't cross these limits. Now you are thinking why I called credit cards are cages? Its simple dear, if you have nothing in your pocket and you can shop $3000, so, you will buy definitely and you have certain day's period interest free. You can pay it in installments. Usually we forget to settle loans in between these interest free period days and we pay interest, interest means if interest rate is just 10%, you have to pay 300 more on 3000, this is a trap, you trap in it and you pay more and more, some countries interest rate is 20 or 30% you can imagine how much additional money they will pay. Banks always say welcome to every person. It doesn't a matter how poor he is. We spend money without any hesitation so we forget it about additional charges and payments. If you have no card, can you buy? Answer is No. without money purchasing could be critical if you have no permanent job or source of income. Make sure about your incomes and then buy from credit cards. If you have less cash inflows then please avoid to use credit cards. To break this habit,

- Use only when your need is so important like food or paying bills.
- Don't keep credit card when you have no need of shopping because it's our nature to be attracted by things and we have a want and demand to buy.
- Pay out your monthly bills with month end or at salary

18. Not Handshake with All

In my office different branches have huge number of staff, few branches have 30+ staff, and 20+ is average staff. When I was at my last designation. I handshake to all staff when I go to any branch. In my city and country it's a social norm to handshake with all. When I got promotion and my designation changed, I continued this habit. Few colleagues said me don't handshake to all, it's not necessary, meet and talk to whom you need to talk. I don't accepted suggestion of my colleagues. I had no idea about western culture because I live and worked only here not with western people. Once I have chance to go Dubai, one of my best friend is working in a multinational company at Dubai. I was so excited to see western people and culture, I decided to visit his office. I went with him, my friend introduce me with all his colleagues, and I chatted with all. I said him for one more day visit of office, second day we went early in morning, I notices all employees shake hand to all, everyone came to me and handshake with me, and it was very good to see it.

I thought, we people are same, we are belong to one city and country, it was my misperception that only I or in our city or country people shake hand with all. We are all same, we are humans. It doesn't means here in my city and country all people shake hand with all. I feel bad if I don't hand shake anyone in office or at a gathering. And I also feel bad when someone hand shake with only few and not with all.

If you have this habit, beak it with keep in mind that, all humans are like me, all need attention, love and care. I respect to someone, he returns too.

19. Color Combination

Have you seen an executive in Baby Pink color suit? It will look weird. Few people I have seen wearing yellow, purple, pink orange color suits. They simply say they don't care people. Yes they are right. Where you are and who you are so important questions in selecting colors. On holidays you may wear any type of color and dress, it doesn't a matter. In corporate world, you have a capacity and worth, may be eyes are observing you as a new employee in their organization. So, it's important to wear good color combination. I had no idea about color combination and I faced some issues in my life in very important events. We will learn how to select and apply good color combinations. Few tips are below

- Its highly recommended, Tie should be with Plain color shirts, we may wear with check too, but like in interviews and corporate meetings, avoid check shirts and tie with check shirt
- In day time meetings, wear light colors like, light gray, beige, off white, earthy shades, if you want to go in night you should wear dark colors like, Navy Blue, black, charcoal, dark gray
- Select tie colors also according to your suit color, if sui color is light, select light color tie
- Don't wear colors like, Pink, lemon, Peach, purple. Don't look like a salad bowl

20. Majority is Authority

We shop according to trend, in shopping centers we buy according to people buy, if a particular product is selling rapidly, majority of customers are taking it in carts, and we include it in our cart too. Its human psychology, most of organizations play a drama with customers, market penetration is not as easy as it pronounced. Company pay people for this drama, they buy from company money, and return products to company and get a commission or wages for doing this. Companies want to penetrate in market and it's very difficult for new product to capture attention of it switch customer from other product to it. If you are satisfied with product you are using, then no need to change. Huge discounts and coupons are included if you buy in bulk and when you buy in bulk and you don't like it, definitely you lose your money. If you have this weird habit, you break it with

- Don't focus on people, purchase like you do
- Don't try to change your mind if you are satisfied, don't experiment and lose money
- If you want to try a new product, buy only unit, don't see discounts and coupons

21. Cleaning Clutter, Arranging Objects

Desks and desktop screens are full of objects, why? It's simply happens when we try to do work for just finishing. If we have to email a particular data, we save file on desktop because it's easy to find and attach from desktop, after email we forget to move or delete it from desktop, similarly items increase day by day and our screen full with files. Similarly our tables and desks getting full day by day with documents and files, we face problem when we try to find a particular file from too many files. We lose time. Arranging objects according to order is an art. It's not difficult and anyone can easily understand it. If you have this weird habit like I had, you can easily break it with keep in mind few tips.

- Make files of documents
- File every document according to its nature, department and importance
- Arrange files according to need, if you need some files on daily basis then keep these on table, files and documents you need once in a month place in a cabinet or locker
- Don't leave desk with files on desk, restore all files on their places

22. Talking during Movies

Movies are like girlfriends, movies want attention. One important dialogue missed, you missed whole movie. Movies are best way to understand people and life. I like to watch movies, I want to learn from movies. If someone talks in between movies, it's a weird habit. It's very bad for movie watching people because they disturb and won't understand movie. Commenting and discussing about a dialogue and scene during movie, divert attention from movie to that talking person, people want to listen hero not that person who is walking. May be people become angry in such situations. If you have this weird habit, don't worry, you can easily break it

- Eat bubble gum during movies, bubble gums keep your mouth busy
- Try to understand movies, discuss at the end of movie with your friends, show them your attention and ability of observations
- Try to take faults from scenes and dialogues, this thing make you so special among people according to your intelligence, but don't do it when you are watching it first time because you won't enjoy movie if you try to find faults, do it when you are watching same movie again.

23. Starting Activities Simultaneously

When I was in college, I needed more money to meet my expenses. I tried to find a job, I was inexperienced, so, I got job of a teacher, in morning I go to school for my job and in evening I went for my education. After 6 months I was failed in examination. It was so worst movement of my life because I was very good student at my school, I got 2nd or 3rd position in my classes during school education. I can't tell you, how much I was sad on that time. I was very shocked and thought how I tell this to my parents. I came home and told to my parents, my parents became very angry and they just said, be serious about your education and life. I started analysis of my mistakes. I list down all my activities on a paper and I found that, I was not studying at home, I only studying at my institute. My schedule was

- ✓ Wake up in morningand go to school for job
- ✓ Come to home, take lunch
- ✓ Go to institute for my education
- ✓ Come home at night
- ✓ Take dinner and sleep, because to tiredness due to whole day working and traveling
- ✓ Wake up next morning and go to school

No time for my education at home, no time for study at home. I left job on very next day, I started studying at home, I passed exam with high marks, I learned a lesson, don't do 2 jobs if you can't handle your day to day tasks. Most people take 2 different courses in 2 different institutions and they failed in both because they can't handle both properly. If you need job and education on same time, do both but make sure you give proper time to your books and study, make a schedule and see how much time can you give to study, if you can't give proper time to study please don't do job, try to do other type of work, in which you have time for study

24. Clicking Pen

According to psychology, clicking pen is a cause of a tension or fear. During meetings managers do it, managers with not satisfactory performance do it more. Students in exams and class do it more when teacher started question from class students, students have fear of not telling right answer and they do clicking pen, clicking pen sound is not good for class room and meetings environment, if you have this weird habit, break it by following steps

- Don't buy pens have button for clicking
- Don't keep pen in your hand when you are not writing
- Keep pen in bag or geometry box, because you have to take and put in it again and again and you won't it frequently

25. Naked at Home

We come in world without clothes, thousands years ago we lived in jungle naked. Being naked is a state of freedom from all type of barriers. We want freedom. Due to our society forms we can't be naked at public places, on beaches we are almost naked but our private parts covered. Nude beaches, nude clubs are exist in our society, but these places are hidden and only naked people wants to go there. According to a survey, 17% of Americans sleep naked, it means 1 out of 6 American sleep naked. In every country and city many number of people sleep naked. It's not a weird habit, it's our state of mind, weird it when we naked at home in day time. in day time, may be you could caught by someone, if you like to be naked at home, be sure, all doors and windows closed, don't use headphones for listening because you won't hear sound of knocking and may be your family reach home and you have no idea about them.

26. Mobile in Meeting

Mom: hellooooo are you listening me ????
Son suddenly see mom and say, yes mom
Mom: tell me what I am talking about
Son have no answer about this question, because son is addictive to cellphone and he was using cellphone while her mom was talking to him, nowadays cellphones are cells, cells in which we are living, we can't easily come outside from these cells. Our social media is rapidly growing day by day, billions of peoples are online and you can easily contact and talk with anyone within few minutes and can meet him with thousands miles away from him. Socially we are not growing, we are neglecting our values. It's a weird habit to use mobile phone in meeting or during talking with someone. It shows lack of interest and respect, it means your conversation is not important for me so, I am busy in cellphone, how to break this weird habit? Wear flap pocket shirts with buttons, put cell in it and don't put outside till conversation ends, put cellphone on charging when mom or dad talking with you, powered off cellphone when you are in a meeting, not bring cellphone in important meetings

27. Buying Before Black Friday

Black Friday started from America and now in whole world. It started in 1952, it was the 4th Thursday of November to Sunday. In black Friday period, huge discounts offers and sales promotions companies offer, people have advantage to buy products at very low prices and can save money. Black Friday is more beneficial if you have to buy electronics and other expensive items because you don't purchase them every months and you buy once in a year. Buying TV before black Friday is losing money, list down items you need to change this year or you have to buy in October or November, don't buy these items and wait for black Friday, buy them on black Friday and save your money

28. Not shaving daily

In corporate world, your mind and body both decide your worth. Mind gives you more and more ideas to do well, body gives you better look, better appearance, shaving daily in a good habit of a gentleman, it's necessary to shave daily when you are in corporate world. Professionals shave daily, others don't. If you are not shaving daily and foreign delegations or other officials meet you, may be they don't think good for you if you not shaved on that day or time. Most people have skin problems and they don't shave daily and most have thick hairs like I have, in these both situations I give you a simple tip. You can easily shave daily after applying this tip.

Take bath as you taken by shower, wash your face as you wash with facewash or soap in during bath, after taking shower and bath. Apply shaving foam on face and shave, you will easily shave because after taking shower and facewash, your face skins and hairs become soft and easy to shave, shaving foam make them softer and you can easily shave daily.

29. Try to Park in Small Space

Gaming and real world have some limitations. In gaming you have no worries about loss in terms of damages and injuries so your fear factor is very less and you take risks and play with more passion and confidence. In real life you won't drive car on highway at speed of 200 miles per hour, you know many other cars are running with you on same road so, you speed down and when road is completely empty then you may be speed up and drive at high speed, because you know about accidents and damage of car and injury or your body. Games are games and you can do whatever you like, playing parking games are very exciting and play it to improve your parking skills, but in real world it's not an easy game for us. If we have this weird habit of parking in small space, we can easily break it,

- First of all, make sure in your mind, your car helps you in every difficult time when you have to reach to a destiny in very short time, so you should have love and care about it
- When you feel love and respect you won't want to hurt it.
- Always think, you are not in game, you may hurt
- I am not here to prove myself here, say this sentence to yourself when you have to park in small space
- When you feel, you have some difficulty to park in a small space, or you have idea after seeing small space for parking then you have no need to park car in that space, try to find another space

30. Study in Last Days

Due to study and job or other activities, we don't give much time to study. When exams near, we start study and take books. This is not a good practice for as an student. We must give proper time daily to our study, if we want to be succeeding in exams. If we study in last few days before exams, maybe we won't get good marks. This is not a good habit for students, it is not so difficult to break this habit. We should

- Make an study plan for week and month

- Try to complete all tasks and goals of week and month in given time period
- If your job is time consuming and you are not giving proper time to studies due to job, change your job
- Bring books with you on job, if you have some time to study there

31. Smelling own breath after wake up

In morning I did it. I always smell my breathing and try to check smell. I always feel bad but it was my habit to do it. I did it many years. One day I thought about it. I realized that, smell of my breaths always bad in morning because after dinner, I didn't brush my teeth after dinner or before sleeping. Whole night my inner body parts move, these produce separate type of gases due to different chemical reactions. So, breath will be bad in morning. How I broken it? It was not easy to break a habit you have from years. It need proper attention and practice. I tried many techniques but I failed, finally I got an idea, I applied it and succeed. I decided

- It is require to leave bed if I count from 1 to 100 in 30 seconds
- If I fail to count, try again and again, if I do it. I can leave bed
- This exercise diverted my mind from smelling my own breath in morning,
- Write on both sides of your hand before sleep, count 1 to 100, it's a reminder if you forget to count and put your hand on mouth, when you see it, definitely you count it

32. Arguments for thinking, not for saying

Debates are part of our lives. We debate in office, college and at home on different issue. My mom want blue color car, my dad likes black color car. They both argue on purchasing of car but being a family member, I join this debate and I will give arguments in favor of one and against for other one. If parents not decided color and arguments go in next day conversations, I think and decide to argue on color black or blue, I try to find some demerits of blue or black colors; I decide my key points and want to say in next day conversation on dinner. When I talk at dining table, my argues are changed, I am saying other points and I decided others. Why and how it happens? Generally, our mind changes statements and words due to situation and we change our point of view if we have listen and see another point about it. So, we change our words and statements. It's a human nature but If I and my mom decide to say some argues about black color and we agree to say some predefined points, if I agree on it and when I change it my mom will not be happy, because I was committed to her. If I change my points, my act will be weird for my mom, if we do like it, we lose confidence and friendship or relationship. It counts in trust. Trust is necessary for any relationship. To break this habit, Write your arguments and try to memories and keep in mind I won't include other words and points in it. Try to take a small card in your hand we you are debating and see card and talk, when you see card your mind will only follow instructions or points of cards and you won't say any other statement

33. Adding Sugar in Green Tea

Green or herbal tea is very helpful to our body, it helps to live well. Green tea is mostly use for weight losing. Green or herbal tea use to weight loses not to use for getting taste. We add sugar in green tea to make its taste better but we lose its benefits because sugar increase weight. It is so weird if we add sugar in green or herbal tea. Green tea is like a medicine not an ordinary tea we take for taste. Medicine has bad taste and we have to take medicine without adding sugar in it. Reason of adding sugar in green tea is, we don't consider it as a medicine, we take it as a tea and we need taste in tea or coffee so we add sugar in it. If you have this weird habit of adding sugar in green tea. You can break it by keeping in your mind that it is a medicine not a tea. A medicine you boil and take in cup. Change your perception about green tea. Take it like a medicine.

34. Talking to Yourself

When I give a test or examination I talk to myself, I talk with my natural voice and this noise is not suitable for class room environment. In addition, I usually talked myself in other situations too. While shopping, walking, working in office I do it. Once I was noticed by my boss, he asked me, to whom I am talking, I replied, to myself. He asked, why? I said, I don't know. He told me that its look so weird when you talk to yourself in front of anyone and may be other person feel uncomfortable by your this weird habit. I apologize to him and ensured him to break this habit soon. I read books and articles on internet, after long study I found few tips and exercises to break it.

- When you start talking to yourself, think and imagine about people are seeing you. It doesn't a matter you are alone. Fell you among people. People are seeing you, you are doing weird
- When you started talking, you start to think in mind and try to talk to yourself without loud voice. talk with your brain and heart

- Self-talk should be for few situations, not for all. Set your activities, which easily allows you to talk like, while reading, gardening, bathing e-t-c. try to don't talk while doing other activities.
- Make conversations, when you alone, you talk to yourself. Try to talk with your family members and office colleagues or class fellows.
- Keep busy, when we busy, we don't think and talk about other activities and things. Keep you busy in different activities like reading, listening music, watching movies, playing games and other activities. When you have time start reading or watching TV.

35. Books for Buying, Not for Reading

I have many books in hardcopy and softcopy. I have huge collection of books on many topics. I buy and download books but not read all. I finish few books in months and buying too many. Why I am doing this? Answer is very simple, thousands of bestsellers are writing books and every day or week some best books published and due to author and subject I buy these books because I love books, I do a job of 10 hours a day and traveling time to office and home is 120 minutes from one side or you can say 2 hours I take to reach office and 2 hours from office to home so I need 4 hours traveling. 10 4=14, 14 hours from day are for my job. Remaining 10 hours are for sleep, social life, shaving, bathing, TV and reading. So, I can't read books daily. I read on weekends but on weekends I spend much time in social gatherings so I don't give proper time to reading and my collection is increasing day by day and I am not finishing books as quick as I am buying. This is a weird habit for me and I break it with some tips and exercises

- Don't buy more than 5 books a month, because we can read a book in a week if we give proper time to it.
- List all books you have, separate books you have to read and try to finish one by one book.
- Don't start a new book without finishing a book, if you are reading a book, finish it and then start new book.
- Make a target to finish your all books in a certain time like month, year or whatever you decide. Don't buy books in that time period and try to finish all books you have to read.

36. Food Battle

Some food combinations are not beneficial for us. Foods have different type of sugars, carbohydrates and proteins, so, these need similar types, and if we take different type of combinations we won't easily digest or take benefits. Have you noticed eating banana with milk is not good for your digestion and sleep patterns? Research shows banana milk shake is not good for our digestion and maybe we can't sleep properly. we eat fruit after meal, we don't get benefits of it because fruit sugars are quickly digest and these sugars won't stay long in body, and if we eat it after food having artificial sugars so you can't digest fruit sugars and after a certain period you lose these sugars and you won't get much benefit from it. It's so weird if we eat and don't get any benefit and get more trouble. This is happens due to our lack of knowledge. We have to search and list all such food combination may harm to us and try to avoid these combinations of food. It's very simple, just spend 1 hour on internet and find these combinations and note in your diary and whenever you decided to eat any food, just look once on diary and eat. You will definitely get more benefits.

37. Name things we use

If someone says you in office to give his baby to him. You will be shocked and look in room for baby. What are you saying dear? Oh sorry I am talking about my cell phone. Kindly take it and give me. Yes, we name objects and things we love and like. It's our affection and love. Generally our attachment with these objects and things give us right to name. It's not a weird habit but in public when we call these by name may be it looks weird and may be people laugh or feel strange about us. If you have this habit and want to break it, simply you don't talk to these things and especially when you alone. When you start to talk to a thing, your attachment increase day by day and your love will increase day by day and you want to call it with a good and lovely name so, you name it.

38. Touching with both

This is one of the weirdest habit I ever had, when I touched with a thing like table, chair or bed with my right hand, I touched my left hand it to make a balance. During walking on road when I touched a stone, I touch it with my other foot too. I did it every day and mostly people seeing me and they asked me about reason. I told them that I want equality and justice with my body. I was very habitual. One day I decided to break this habit, it was one of the difficult task of my life and I read a lot for it and discussed to people. After long time working I found some practices and tips to break this habit. This is a mind game and strategy, if your mind and your self believe is strong you may soon break it.

- Believe about universal energies and forces, all things, people or places you see or touch are according to a universal order

- When someone come to you and put hand on your right shoulder it means it's a universal energy that giving instruction to put hand on right not on left
- If you touch with your right hand means universal energies selected your right hand instead of left hand so, this is not for left hand
- When you have this believe strong you never use your other hand or foot for touching because you have a believe about universal order of things

I take about 1 year to break this habit, I hope you will break soon if you develop your believe early.

39. Listening Music while working

Music is very helpful to our emotions and feelings; we get benefit of music when we listen it with attention. If we listen it during a gathering of people or in very noisy market, we won't get benefit of it. Yes, we listen it but it won't be fruitful for us. If we work on excel sheet, we need proper attention because we are doing some sensitive working related to data processing and each and every formula we put on cell, we verify again and again to be ensure about accuracy of data. If we put earphones while doing working on excel sheet, we won't get taste and result of music because we don't have proper attention to singer, quality of voice, lyrics and music. It's a weird habit and it is useless for us because we have only focus on our working not on song, singer, lyrics and music. To break this habit never put earphone in your pocket or bag when you go to office. You haven't so you can't play music in office without earphones.

40. Talking to Things

Talking to things is a useless activity, we are social. We need to talk but we should to talk to people not to things. It looks weird if I talk to my watch and ask time. Will watch tell me time? Will watch give me any gesture or expression? No. I don't need to talk to things because we are more than 7 billion people on planet earth; these are enough for me to talk. Why we talk to things? Main reason of this habit is our love affection to things and our loneliness. If I have no close or best friends, I don't want to share my feelings and secrets to people. I search good friends in things and objects. Second factor is trust factor, many be my friend lose trust but things won't. When we feel loneliness and want to share our feeling and some secrets we try to talk to ourselves or to things and slowly we develop this habit is us. It looks so weird when we talk to a glass or bottle in a party. If we have this weird habit, we can easily break it

- be social, make friends in office, college, neighbors or on social media
- Try to talk to 5 people in a day, without meeting them. I mean talk them on call
- Attend all social gatherings and parties you invited
- When you alone and you feel to talk to your pen or cell phone, post your status or tweet on social media. Post on social media instead of talking to things

41. Holding Glass for Long Time

On table during dinner, we have glass of water in our hand and are busy in discussion and we don't drink for a long time. It is also happens when we have cup of tea too. We don't put it on table and don't drink it. It seems we are hired for taking glass or keeping in our hand. When we are involved in discussions we pay more attention on it and we forget about glass or cup in our hand and we continuously listening and seeing people talking, we don't drink because if we have to talk suddenly or promptly give reaction or reply then maybe we won't do it if we are drinking on that time. it looks weird because all people are sitting after finishing and only you have cup or glass of water in hand and you are listening and talking to people. We can easily break this habit, keep in mind that I will join discussion after finishing my dinner or lunch, finish all things you have to eat and drink then join discussion.

42. Criticize Everything

We don't like many people in our life according to their policies, habits. Maybe we have close relationship with them or we live and work with them. It's our nature to comment and criticize on politicians and leaders. We like and appreciate our party politicians and leaders and we criticize to our opposite party members, leaders and politicians. We have in mind that we only have to appreciate our party and criticize to opposite party. We don't see our party mistakes and we neglect best policies or practices of opposite party. It's weird if our opposite party gives a good economic plan and we refuse or criticize it and if our party gives a bad economic plan and we appreciate and welcome it. Why we do it, because it's our nature we like and love our favorite persons and we won't want to listen and see mistakes of them and we believe they won't make a mistake or do bad. Being a citizen it's our duty to think and do well to our country. If we have this weird habit, we can easily break it. Make your rules and strictly follow

- Keep in mind, you have to justice with your country
- It's your duty to appreciate whatever is best for your country, it doesn't a matter who is doing it
- Loss of country is our loss, protest and resist bad policies that give loss to country

43. Brushing Teeth for long Time

I brushed 20 minutes when I was in 10; I don't know why I did it. Most of time I reach late to school but I did it every day. When I become a professional and stared a job I brush for 15 minutes. Now, I brush for 5 minutes. Reason of this habit is I have stain on my tooth by birth. I had in my mind that may be I washout it by brushing more and more. I tried many brands of tooth paste but I failed. This weird habit is common in people who believe in hygiene and want to live healthy life. Brushing long time is not a bad habit but it looks weird if you brush in front of your family member or roommate for long time. You can break this habit easily, divide your time in different sections of day like morning, evening and before sleep. If you give 7 minutes each time, you will brush 21 minutes whole day and you clean your teeth 2 times more.

44. Watching same movie/Episode again and again

La Tigre e la neve (Tiger and the snow) is my favorite movie. Its story, cast and dialogues are awesome and I like to watch it again and again. I watch it 20 times and still want to watch it again and again. Once I was watching it and my sister asked about it, I told her about story and movie. Next night I was watching again and my sister again asked about it. She said, you were watching it yesterday. I said yes. She said why? I had no answer and I said actually I missed last part yesterday so I am watching. On third day she noted me again and she was shocked and asked why you are watching it again and again. I had no answer and I just said to her, I like it. She said that why you are wasting your time on this movies, you once watched then watch another movies or to do other activity. I was so embarrassed and closed movies window, shut down system and slept. I felt weird and decided to break this habit. Reason behind this habit is our likeness and love to particular movie or episode and we want to watch it again and again I study books and articles on internet and found some tips about it.

- Delete movie from your PC or Cell phone if you watched it
- If you have DVD, place it on very above place in your home, or place it in last because you need to put all DVDs and then set again all so, this time consuming activity stops you to take it out and watch it.
- Make a list of movies and set a target to watch all them before a certain time, you won't see again and again same movies if you have to finish other movies.

45. Reading Shampoo Back Cover under shower

While taking shower, I read shampoo back cover and it was weird but I did it many times. Mostly I was unable to read words and numbers due to water drops but I tried my best to read. I used same brand for years but when I used new bottle I started to read label, instructions and ingredients. Reason of it was so simple, I was brand conscious and I read and research before buying things. On the time of buying shampoo I read label and cover but at the time of shower I look again. I wanted to ensure about product features and ingredients. It wasted my time in morning and I spent 5 minutes on just reading label. I broke this habit very easily, on store I read label before buying and after coming to home I removed shampoo label and back cover and placed it in bathroom.

46. Check then Leave Home

Most of us check road, street and surroundings then leave home. May be it's due to our security concern or risk of theft or uncertainty. It is more dangerous if you give a gesture like it to strangers and criminals because your suspicious gestures make you and your house more notable. Please don't do this weird habit. To break this habit, check your windows and doors properly and close them, make ensure about they before leaving home, keep in mind that your suspicious gestures may make trouble for you. When you leave your home, stand on door and place your head inside for few seconds then shut the main door and leave house. When you put your head inside door, people think you are talking to someone inside the house and no one won't try to enter home due to availability of someone at home

47. Sleeping at Parties

One of my best friend has this habit, he sleeps during parties. Mostly parties starts very late and end after mid night, people who have habit of wake up too early, feel much tiredness after mid night and they want to sleep at any cost. They put head on sofa and start sleeping. It looks weird, people don't know about your life style and sleeping timings they just laugh on you. If you want to break your this habit, make sure about party timing, if party is too late, avoid to go there or leave party when you feel uncomfortable and excuse and leave party. If you want to be part of party, take tea or coffee, wash your face with cold water specially your eyes. Come home from office then try to sleep or lay down on bed and take a rest. It will help your body to be fresh and active at night during party.

48. Examine Money

Many people have fear of cheating or fruad. People check currency bills and notes again and again and ensure about it. It is easy when you check dollar bill offered by a stranger but if he is your family member or relative, it would be so weird because he thinks that you have no trust on him so, you are checking again and again dollar bill. This is a weird habit and maybe he feel bad for it. If you have habit of checking dollar bills again and again and checking all bills, you need to buy a ultraviolet rays pen or device. It will show you certain marks on dollar bill, if bill is genuine . you just put light of pen once on dollar bill and keep it in pocket and no need to count again and again. It will save your time and reduce chance of fake currency

49. Forget spelling of simple words

If spelling check doesn't exist, maybe I can't write this book or paragraph easily and properly. I forget spellings of simple words like than and then have huge difference but mostly I use than instead of then most times and few other words too. This is not good for a writer or employee specially when we sit in a test and grammar or English section become very difficult for us and we lose job just because of few grammar and spelling mistakes. When we get result and we examiner asked about our qualification. We feel so embarrassment to tell him how much we study. Reason behind this weird habit is our lack of interest, we don't focus on things as we should do. To break this habit we should write these words again and again with meaning and we make sentences of these words. Make 10 sentences of every word we have confusion or we don't know proper spelling, practice makes perfect. Practice needs time but ten sentences don't need much time. We can improve 5 words per day easily and 150 in a month. Write list of all words you need to correct spelling or correct use, practice one by one word and mark them. Randomly check your knowledge by using these words in sentences or by typing them in word file.

50. Extra Kind on Social Media

We usually be kind and good on social media, it's our nature to be good and to look good when we are in crowd. It's a good nature of us and we do well when we are in public. Social media is now everywhere, majority of our population use social media to express themselves and participate in virtual gatherings and parties. We show us extra kind on social media, because we want to build our good image to our virtual friends. We try to make people happy, help to people and offer all services to our virtual friends. We forget or limitations and continue offer and serve without any idea. I started social media in 2009 and I was doing job. Once few students asked me about economics and I satisfied them with my answers and way of teaching. They appreciate me a lot and requested me to teach them. I was so social and extra kind on social media. So, I agreed to teach them. On these days my office was too far from home, it was 55 Km from my home and lack of public transport on that route make my traveling more worst and time consuming. I reach home at 7:30 or 8:00 PM and my job was based on field work. I was traveling 3 hours for going to offlce and come back to home; in addition I travelled more due to my nature of job. When I reached home I was too tired and wanted to sleep. When I reached home I login and watch notifications, all students were waiting for me and asking different questions in my inbox. I was kind and committed to them so, I teach them answer them. It was too time consuming for me. I gave 3 to 4 hours to them. I was very disturbed but I was committed to them so I was completing my responsibility. After examination of them. I stopped social media for few weeks. I realized that my life is getting tough day by day and I am not giving proper time to my family and my life. I decided to leave social media completely. I stopped social media and enjoyed my life. After few months I login and I was so shocked to see messages in inbox, my students were requesting me again for next class and other people requesting me to teach them. I replied to all one by one and excuse them. I said them that I can't manage my time and can't give you proper attention. They were disappointed. It was very bad movement for me to refuse them. I learned a lesson from social media that, help people, offer services but don't be too kind and hero. This was my weird habit and I broke it with my own decision. If you have this habit you just need to think

- You are not a superman
- You have limitations
- You have your family and personal life
- You have to take complete rest and doing all activities then you have to serve for others

51. Use Both Hands to drink a Glass or Water

Have you watched President Donald Trump, the way he drinks water? He takes glass in his both hands and drinks it like a 4 years old child does. Donald Trump is not only person on this planet is doing this. Many of us do it. It looks weird because we are not children and we can take glass by one hand. We don't need both hands to take it. Why we do it. Few things in life are difficult to define. We do without any reason. Holding with two hands and taking it with two hands shows our possessiveness and risk of dropping glass from our hand. Maybe it is due to our any past incident, when we dropped our glass and we have a fear in our mind, if we hold it with both hands it will be safe in our hands. If you have this weird habit and you want to break it. Just think you are not a 4 years old child and you are confident to take things properly. After developing your believe in mind that you are not a child, do this exercise. Fill completely glass with water and hold it in one hand and walk 20 steps. Water level should be same after walking. In this exercise you will walk with care and attention, so this exercise will develop habit of attention and care whenever you take glass of water in your hand.

52. Laughing without any reason

Hahahahahaha, when you do it suddenly at office or home, people see you and ask you, why you are laughing loudly, what happens. If you say nothing, without any reason I am laughing. I guarantee you, all will laugh at you because laughing without any joke or funny thing is weird. We do it sometimes and we laugh loudly. When we alone its ok with this habit. In public we have to control ourselves from laughing without any reason. Our mind sometimes think random things from our past and when a funny movement comes in our mind for few seconds, we start laughing and we forget about it, what we seen or thought. How to break this weird habit? When you laughing,

- Pinch your
- Make list in mind of activities remaining
- Start to find red or blue color in room
- Counting backward from 10 to 1

53. **Not Replying to Phone Calls**

Why we take cell phone? Why we have cell phone? Why we use cell phone? What is basic function of cell phone? Mostly answers of these questions will be, for communication. Communication is a two way process of exchanging our thoughts, ideas and messages. If we stop communicating by cell phone, the purpose of having it will be changed. Few people have this weird habit, they don't attend calls. They call back or text after few hours and ask for reason of calling them. They have many disadvantages due to this weird habit, like if they have a call from a employer or any relative of them needs immediately help. They don't get informed. Reason behind this habit is maybe we are celebrities and we have no time for attending calls, maybe we think we are so important and busy for other people. To break this habit you just need to do this activity, make a sheet, at the end of every day you check your cell phone and count number of calls you received and total number of incoming calls. Take percentage of it. Set a target of 50% calls you should have to receive in first week, 60% in next week and increase 10% every week. When we challenge us and accept a challenge, we put all efforts and try to complete it. This challenge will break this weird habit within 1 month of time if you properly do this exercise.

54. **Licking before Eating**

Many people lick creamy biscuits before eat them, they want to taste cream. After licking they east biscuit. Few of us lick ketchup and other sauces from food items then eat it. It looks too weird, maybe people feel so bad and leave your table. We are 7 billion people on earth; everyone has his own choices and everyone want to do according to his thinking. For taste it's a good way to lick but in public its very weird. We want to taste separately so we do it. If you want to break this habit, you need to keep in your mind about taste of whole item at once. In other words you can say, taste all ingredients once. For example if you are eating burger, try to get taste of bun, cheese, chicken, mayonnaise and ketchup at same time. You will definitely like it because all ingredients make new and better taste. Food companies and restaurants spend huge money on research and developing new taste due to cut throat competition in market. They make products more and more tasty and unique so, enjoy products as they packed and served to you.

55. Buying Small Size of Shoes, They look better

Most of people buy small size of shoes, they think they look better in small size shoes, because if you have long feet, may be you look weird. Small size shoes look better but disadvantage of these shoes is shape and comfort of your feet may change. Maybe you get problems in walking and running. Fashion and style conscious people have this habit. If you want to break this habit. Focus on your comfort and shape of your feet. Comfort means relax. Follow the rule of shape and comfort, you never want to compromise on shape and comfort so, you won't buy small size shoes.

56. Wearing 2 watches, Holding 2 Cell phones

I have seen few people with 2 watches and 2 or 3 cell phones. Dual sim cell phones are available in market. Smart watches are also available in market. So, why they doing it. It looks weird when we wear 2 or 3 watches in 1 hand and walk in public.

Keeping 2 or 3 Smartphone is also weird. Reason of this habit is maybe they want to show number of watches or cell phones they have, or maybe they have to check different times of different time zones. May be they are addict to cell phones and they are keeping extra cell phone as a backup. If one cell phone battery downs they have other for use. These are few reason behind this weird habit. To break this habit, wear a smart watch and install time zone app. You don't need to wear 2 or 3 watches. If you have fear of battery life of cell phone. Buy portable charger or power bank. If you are using 2 cell phones due to 2 different cellular operators, use a dual sim Smartphone or cell phone.

57. After reading few pages, saying I read whole Book

When we talk about a book, in a gathering or at party, few of us claims that they read whole book. We feel glad if a book we like and others like it too. Sometimes in such situations, people ask about a certain chapter or character. It is so embarrassing movement if we claim about reading whole books and we can't answer to him. This is also happens we talk about movies. We just watch few scenes of movie and interpret whole story from these scenes. We also extract central idea of whole book by reading few pages of book reviews. We forget, anyone may ask a different question and we will face trouble in public. It is easy to avoid this practice by not involving in such conversations, if you must have to talk in such conversations, try to talk about writer, not about book because you can easily define writer instead of whole book, and say I started his book but due to my schedule I read only few pages and talk only about these pages.

58. Saying twice at call, saying Loudly

Dad: Complete your homework

Son: yes daddy

Dad: please complete it then go to play

Son: yes daddy

This is an example of saying twice on call. We are not confirmed about the person we are talking. He is listening with attention or not. We feel and believe Face to face talk is very clear and powerful instead of call or text. We talk with loud voice because we feel, other person maybe not listening us properly or with attention. This doubt makes us weird on calls and we act different as we don't normally. To break this habit. We need to understand nature of person to whom we are talking on phone. If he is careless and dull person so we can say sentences and words twice with loud voice. If other side person is a caring and good person and we talk twice and loud. It would be weird. Understand person while talking. If person is good, don't say twice because you know he can understand well.

59. Change Plan

Think and imagine if you are going to camping , you are so exciting and making plans in your mind and suddenly your team leader or organizer cancel plan of camping and go to beach for swimming. What you feel in this situation. Maybe you argue him and maybe you fight with him. It is so weird when someone changes plan suddenly without any reason. Why someone do it. When he has choices and other options in mind and when he realized this destination or activity is not better as to other, he move to other. Second reason is when he wanted to go to an specific destination and other group members refused it. He need to go there at any cost. He definitely change plan. To break this weird habit you need to know value of friends and precious movements. Life is short, enjoy it with friends and you don't know about your future job, town and country. Enjoy movements with friends and you never enjoy if only you enjoy activity and others don't. It's win-win situation. Be happy, make happy.

60. Forget to switch off TV

Few of us sleep without switch off TV. Due to tiredness we unaware most of time when we close eyes and asleep during watching TV. This is weird when we are living with family or roommates. We do it mostly every night. It is easy to break this habit. Set a timer in TV and at a certain time TV will automatically switch off.